# POCKET
# prayers

## 40 SIMPLE PRAYERS THAT
## BRING PEACE AND REST

## MAX LUCADO

### with *Andrea Lucado*

THOMAS NELSON
*Since 1798*

NASHVILLE   MEXICO CITY   RIO DE JANEIRO

Published in Nashville, Tennessee, by Thomas Nelson, a division of HarperCollins Christian Publishing, Inc.

Thomas Nelson titles may be purchased in bulk for educational, business, fund-raising, or sales promotional use. For information, please e-mail SpecialMarkets@ThomasNelson.com.

Unless otherwise noted, Scripture quotations are taken from the New King James Version®. © 1982 by Thomas Nelson, Inc. Used by permission. All rights reserved.

Other Scripture references are from the following sources: New Century Version® (NCV). © 2005 by Thomas Nelson, Inc. Used by permission. All rights reserved. Holy Bible, New International Version®, NIV® (NIV). © 1973, 1978, 1984, 2011 by Biblica, Inc.™ Used by permission of Zondervan. All rights reserved worldwide. www.zondervan.com. *Holy Bible*, New Living Translation (NLT). © 1996, 2004, 2007. Used by permission of Tyndale House Publishers, Inc., Wheaton, Illinois 60189. All rights reserved.

ISBN 978-0-7180-1404-9

*Printed in the United States of America*

19  20  21  LSC  22  21  20  19  18

# POCKET
# prayers

# The Pocket Prayer

Hello, my name is Max. I'm a recovering prayer wimp. I doze off when I pray. My thoughts zig, then zag, then zig again. Distractions swarm like gnats on a summer night. If attention deficit disorder applies to prayer, I am afflicted. When I pray, I think of a thousand things I need to do. I forget the one thing I set out to do: pray.

Some people excel in prayer. They inhale heaven and exhale God. They are the SEAL Team Six of intercession. They would rather pray than sleep. Why is it that I sleep when I pray? They belong to the PGA: Prayer Giants Association. I am a card-carrying member of the PWA: Prayer Wimps Anonymous.

Can you relate? It's not that we don't pray at all. We all pray some.

On tearstained pillows we pray.

In grand liturgies we pray.

At the sight of geese in flight, we pray.

Quoting ancient devotions, we pray.

We pray to stay sober, centered, or solvent. We pray when the lump is deemed malignant. When the money runs out before the month does. When the unborn baby hasn't kicked in a while. We all pray . . . some.

But wouldn't we all like to pray . . .

More?

Better?

Deeper?

Stronger?

With more fire, faith, or fervency?

Yet we have kids to feed, bills to pay, deadlines to meet. The calendar pounces on our good intentions like a tiger on a rabbit. We want to pray, but *when*?

We want to pray, but *why*? We might as well admit it. Prayer is odd, peculiar. Speaking into space. Lifting words into the sky. We can't even get the cable company to answer us, yet God will? The doctor is too busy, but God isn't? We have our doubts about prayer.

And we have our checkered history with prayer: unmet expectations, unanswered requests. We can barely genuflect for the scar tissue on our knees. God, to some, is the ultimate heartbreaker.

Why keep tossing the coins of our longings into a silent pool? He jilted me once . . . but not twice.

Oh, the peculiar puzzle of prayer.

We aren't the first to struggle. The sign-up sheet for Prayer 101 contains some familiar names: the apostles John, James, Andrew, and Peter. When one of Jesus' disciples requested, "Lord, teach us to pray" (Luke 11:1 NIV), none of the others objected. No one walked away saying, "Hey, I have prayer figured out." The first followers of Jesus needed prayer guidance.

In fact, the only tutorial they ever requested was on prayer. They could have asked for instructions on many topics: bread multiplying, speech making, storm stilling. Jesus raised people from the dead. But a "How to Vacate the Cemetery" seminar? His followers never called for one. But they did want him to do this: "Lord, teach us to pray."

Might their interest have had something to do with the jaw-dropping, eye-popping promises Jesus attached to prayer? "Ask and it will be given to you" (Matt. 7:7 NIV). "If you believe, you will get anything you ask for in prayer"

(Matt. 21:22 NCV). Jesus never attached such power to other endeavors. "*Plan* and it will be given to you." "You will get anything you *work* for." Those words are not in the Bible. But these are—"If you remain in me and follow my teachings, you can ask anything you want, and it will be given to you" (John 15:7 NCV).

Jesus gave stunning prayer promises.

And he set a compelling prayer example. Jesus prayed before he ate. He prayed for children. He prayed for the sick. He prayed with thanks. He prayed with tears. He had made the planets and shaped the stars, yet he prayed. He is the Lord of angels and Commander of heavenly hosts, yet he prayed. He is coequal with God, the exact representation of the Holy One, and yet he devoted himself to prayer. He prayed in the desert, cemetery, and garden. "He went out and departed to a solitary place; and there He prayed" (Mark 1:35).

This dialogue must have been common among his friends:

"Has anyone seen Jesus?"

"Oh, you know. He's up to the same thing."

"Praying *again*?

"Yep. He's been gone since sunrise."

Jesus would even disappear for an entire night of prayer. I'm thinking of one occasion in particular. He'd just experienced one of the most stressful days of his ministry. The day began with the news of the death of his relative John the Baptist. Jesus sought to retreat with his disciples, yet a throng of thousands followed him. Though grief-stricken, he spent the day teaching and healing people. When it was discovered that the host of people had no food to eat, Jesus multiplied bread out of a basket and fed the entire multitude. In the span of a few hours, he battled sorrow, stress, demands, and needs. He deserved a good night's rest. Yet when evening finally came, he told the crowd to leave and the disciples to board their boat, and "he went up into the hills by himself to pray" (Mark 6:46 NLT).

Apparently it was the correct choice. A storm exploded over the Sea of Galilee, leaving the disciples "in trouble far away from land, for a strong wind had risen, and they were fighting heavy waves. About three o'clock in the morning Jesus came toward them, walking on the water" (Matt. 14:24–25 NLT). Jesus ascended the mountain depleted. He reappeared invigorated. When he reached the water, he never broke his stride. You'd have thought the water was a park lawn and the storm a spring breeze.

Do you think the disciples made the prayer–power connection? "Lord, teach us to pray *like that*. Teach us to find strength in prayer. To banish fear in prayer. To defy storms in prayer. To come off the mountain of prayer with the authority of a prince."

What about you? The disciples faced angry waves and a watery grave. You face angry clients, a turbulent economy, raging seas of stress and sorrow.

"Lord," we still request, "teach us to pray."

When the disciples asked Jesus to teach them to pray, he gave them a prayer. Not a lecture on prayer. Not the doctrine of prayer. He gave them a quotable, repeatable, portable prayer (Luke 11:1–4).

Could you use the same? It seems to me that the prayers of the Bible can be distilled into one. The result is a simple, easy-to-remember, pocket-size prayer:

*Father,*

 *you are good.*

  *I need help. Heal me and forgive me.*

  *They need help.*

  *Thank you.*

  *In Jesus' name, amen.*

Let this prayer punctuate your day. As you begin your morning, *Father, you are good.* As you commute to work or walk the hallways at school, *I need help.* As you wait in the grocery line, *They need help.* Keep this prayer in your pocket as you pass through the day.

When we invite God into our world, he walks in. He brings a host of gifts: joy, patience, resilience. Anxieties come, but they don't stick. Fears surface and then depart. Regrets land on the windshield, but then comes the wiper of prayer. The devil still hands me stones of guilt, but I turn and give them to Christ. I'm completing my sixth decade, yet I'm wired with energy. I am happier, healthier, and more hopeful than I have ever been. Struggles come, for sure. But so does God.

Prayer is not a privilege for the pious, not the art of a chosen few. Prayer is simply a heartfelt conversation between God and his child. My friend, he wants to talk with you. Even now, as you read these words, he taps at the door. Open it. Welcome him in. Let the conversation begin.

*For you did not receive the spirit
of bondage again to fear, but you
received the Spirit of adoption by
whom we cry out, "Abba, Father."*

**ROMANS 8:15**

Father, you have made me your child through your Spirit. In your kindness you adopted me and delivered me from sin and death.

Remind me today what it means to be your child and to be free from that law. It is so easy for me to live my day on my own terms. Help me to live it in light of your grace.

I pray for my friends and family. Help them experience your love as their father and feel their inheritance in your spirit.

Thank you for accepting me as I am but not leaving me the same.

In Jesus' name, amen.

## 2

*And because you are sons, God has
sent forth the Spirit of His Son into your
hearts, crying out, "Abba, Father!"*

GALATIANS 4:6

Abba, thank you for sending a helper to
direct my steps. You know everything and
will guide me in your will.

Help me to know your will. Keep me on the
path you have set for me. Give me the desire to
stay true to that path, and forgive me for the
times I have already strayed from you.

Be with my friends and family who are at
a crossroads and don't know what to do next.
May your spirit guide them and make the best
decision clear.

Thank you for caring about the details of my
life, for not believing any request is too small.

I pray this in Jesus' name, amen.

*Our Father in heaven, hallowed be Your
name. Your kingdom come. Your will
be done on earth as it is in heaven.*

MATTHEW 6:9–10

F ather, you are above all, know all, and see
all. Yet you hear me as if I am your only
creation.

May I not view you as a distant father, but as
one who has come to earth and understands the
challenges and temptations of my life. Be near
me today and whisper reminders that you are
close and holding me as your child.

My friends need you today as they make dif-
ficult decisions in their workplaces and within
their families. Would you show them that you
are closer than even their earthly fathers?

Thank you for hearing me and listening to
my pleas.

It's in Jesus' name I pray this, amen.

*Yet for us there is one God, the Father, of whom are all things, and we for Him; and one Lord Jesus Christ, through whom are all things, and through whom we live.*

1 CORINTHIANS 8:6

G od, you are my father who gives all good things. I have life because of you, and there is no one like you.

I ask that you would deepen that truth in my heart today. Point out my idols and the things I worship apart from you, that I would remember you alone are my God.

Give my friends and loved ones freedom from their idols as well so they can fully enjoy being part of your family. Help them know that you are their only creator and nothing on this earth has ownership of them.

Thank you for loving us, your creation, even when we go astray.

In Jesus' name, amen.

*A father of the fatherless, a defender of
widows, is God in His holy habitation.
God sets the solitary in families; He brings
out those who are bound into prosperity.*

PSALM 68:5–6

Dear God, you are the Father to the fatherless. You provide for those without a family
and defend the weak as their own father would.

Today I feel defenseless. When I feel
attacked, would you remind me that you protect
me? Would you be my father and defender today?

Please defend those who are weak and afraid
and feel forgotten. Show up in their lives today
and remind them that they are your children
and you are their heavenly Father.

Thank you for giving me a spiritual family
that can never be taken away.

I pray this in the name of Jesus, amen.

# 6

*For unto us a Child is born, unto us a Son is given; and the government will be upon His shoulder. And His name will be called Wonderful, Counselor, Mighty God, Everlasting Father, Prince of Peace.*

Isaiah 9:6

Everlasting father, you are the mighty God. You sent your Son and performed the final sacrifice, and you deserve all of our praise.

I need your help today. I am a sinner and am feeling the weight of my sin. Show me what your Son's birth means for me in this moment.

Give grace to those who have not accepted your Son and do not know the freedom he gives. Let them see that you are their loving Father.

Thank you for loving me not just yesterday or today but always, no matter the depth of my sin. I am grateful.

In your Son's precious name, amen.

*Good and upright is the LORD; therefore*
*He teaches sinners in the way. The*
*humble He guides in justice, and the*
*humble He teaches His way.*

PSALM 25:8–9

Dear father, you are good. Your ways are perfect and above my own. You deserve my full obedience and my worship. You are my teacher and authority because of your goodness.

Humble me today when I choose my way over yours. Use my prideful moments as an opportunity to teach me and redirect me.

Show my friends that your goodness is more important than their desires. Provide them with encouragement to seek your good and upright way.

Thank you for your constant instruction and concern for each step of my life.

In the name of Jesus I pray these things, amen.

*For to You, O Lord, I lift up my soul.*
*For You, Lord, are good, and ready*
*to forgive, and abundant in mercy*
*to all those who call upon You.*

PSALM 86:4–5

God, you are abounding in forgiveness and mercy and goodness I cannot understand in this life. I worship you with my heart and soul.

As I sit in regret and guilt over past sin, remind me of your forgiveness. Please let me feel your mercy. Fill me with it so I can give it to others I encounter today.

Walk closely with my family so they can know your grace. Lift their burdens and point their faces toward you.

I give you thanks for the grace I do not deserve and your mercies, which are new every morning.

In Christ's name, amen.

*Who being the brightness of His glory
and the express image of His person, and
upholding all things by the word of His
power, when He had by Himself purged our
sins, sat down at the right hand of the Majesty
on high, having become so much better
than the angels, as He has by inheritance
obtained a more excellent name than they.*

HEBREWS 1:3–4

Father, you created all things simply with
your words. One word from you and your
power is evident. I am amazed by you.

I need your power in my life, God. I face
impossible circumstances and am desperate for
a miracle. Would you show me your power in
my life today?

God, for those who have a small view of
you, show them how mighty and enormous you
actually are. Help them to find comfort in that
knowledge.

Thank you for sending your Son, who has
made our relationship with you possible.

It's in the all-powerful name of Jesus that I
pray, amen.

# 10

*Oh, taste and see that the LORD is good;*
*Blessed is the man who trusts in Him!*
*Oh, fear the LORD, you His saints! There*
*is no want to those who fear Him.*

PSALM 34:8

Merciful father, I see that you are good. I fear you and am humbled when I look toward your face. You bless me when I don't deserve it.

Lord, I often feel far from you. Bring me close and remind me what it's like to be in close relationship with you.

Would you be with all those who are lonely right now? Surround them with a loving community and fulfill all their needs.

Thank you that I don't need anything when I am in you.

In the name of Jesus, amen.

*"For I am God, and there is no other; I
am God, and there is none like Me,
declaring the end from the beginning,
and from ancient times things that are
not yet done, saying, 'My counsel shall
stand, and I will do all My pleasure.'"*

ISAIAH 46:9–10

God above, there is no one like you. You are
the one, true God. The only God that I
worship, the Alpha and Omega.

I need to know that you have gone before
me. I see no solution for the problems I'm fac-
ing. Remind me that you are not perplexed by
the struggles I face so that I may be comforted
by your all-knowing power.

Be near to my family and friends who are
suffering. Their pain is paralyzing, but you are
greater than anything they face.

Thank you for your perfect will. May it be
done in my life as I seek you.

In your name alone, amen.

# 12

*Every good gift and every perfect gift*
*is from above, and comes down from*
*the Father of lights, with whom there is*
*no variation or shadow of turning.*

JAMES 1:17

Dear Father, your blessings are perfect. All that you give is good. From creation to the end, your gifts bring life to this earth.

Teach me to accept what you've given. I may not always understand circumstances, but show me how they are blessings and give me gratitude for all of your gifts.

Rain your blessings on my friends and family today. Give them hope whatever they face. May they recognize that the good and perfect gifts are from you.

Thank you that your blessings never end. You give them to us at unexpected times.

In Jesus' name, amen.

> *"O Lord GOD, You are God, and Your
> words are true, and You have promised
> this goodness to Your servant."*

2 SAMUEL 7:28

Almighty God, you speak and it is done. Your words are true. They are powerful and they bring life.

Would you give me a desire for your words? Sometimes I feel anxious but do not turn to scripture. I am fearful yet forget to ask you for protection. I am weak but reluctant to ask you for strength. Renew my desire for your constant help and remind me to return to your Word.

Make your word close to my friends in need today. Please bring to their minds the words they need for encouragement and direction.

Thank you that the Bible is all I need. Thank you for giving it to us as a gift and a guide. May I never take that for granted.

In your name I pray this, amen.

# 14

*Be anxious for nothing, but in everything by*
*prayer and supplication, with thanksgiving,*
*let your requests be made known to God;*
*and the peace of God, which surpasses*
*all understanding, will guard your hearts*
*and minds through Christ Jesus.*

PHILIPPIANS 4:6–7

Dear Father, you are the Prince of Peace and the great I Am. You are my helper and my redeemer.

I need your help today. I am weak and frail and tired. Give me the strength to get through just this day and the desire to work as if I am doing it all for your glory.

Help those who are carrying especially heavy burdens right now. They need your power and peace that goes beyond our understanding.

I am so grateful that I can come to you and present my requests at any time. Thank you for giving me peace and rest even in the hard times.

In the name of the Prince of Peace, I pray, amen.

*Therefore humble yourselves under the
mighty hand of God, that He may exalt
you in due time, casting all your care
upon Him, for He cares for you.*

1 PETER 5:6–7

Dear God, you are above all and worthy is
your name.

I humbly come before you, confessing that I
am a sinner. What I have done deserves justice
and not grace, but I need to feel your grace today.
I need your forgiveness. Would you replace the
guilt, replace the shame I feel?

Be near to my friends and family who have
secret shame they are afraid to reveal. May you
give them a trusted friend and confidant and a
sense of your forgiveness in their lives.

Thank you for taking our cares and burdens upon yourself. Thank you for promising
to always care for each of us.

In Jesus' name, amen.

# 16

*They said to Him, "Lord, that our eyes may be opened." So Jesus had compassion and touched their eyes. And immediately their eyes received sight, and they followed Him.*

MATTHEW 20:33–34

Father, you are the Healer and Miracle Maker. You can give sight to the blind and a voice to the voiceless.

Would you heal my body? I am in pain and need the healing only you can give. Give me an optimistic outlook despite my weaknesses.

For my family, please bring them miraculous healing in body and mind. Strengthen their faith and encourage them.

I thank you that you always hear my cries for help.

I pray this in the name of the great Healer, amen.

*Now may the God of peace Himself sanctify
you completely; and may your whole spirit,
soul, and body be preserved blameless at the
coming of our Lord Jesus Christ. He who
calls you is faithful, who also will do it.*

1 THESSALONIANS 5:23–24

Dear God, your faithfulness is sure and steady. Your being is whole and complete. When I feel incomplete, like there are holes in me, I try and fill them with things that are not of you. But you have called me to something greater. Show me what that is and allow me to find fulfillment in you.

Protect my friends' hearts who have been in destructive relationships. They feel broken and frightened. Mend their wounds and give them peace.

I give thanks for your faithfulness. It is my rock. When everything feels shaky like sand, thank you for being solid.

In Jesus' name, amen.

# 18

*But He was wounded for our transgressions,*
*He was bruised for our iniquities; the*
*chastisement for our peace was upon*
*Him, and by His stripes we are healed.*

ISAIAH 53:5

Father God, you redeem me from my sin. You have taken it far away from me. You are perfect love.

Help me as I search to find worth. I feel so unworthy of love at times, and I need your help to discover where my true worth is.

Be strength for my friends who don't believe their sin is taken care of and are walking around with unnecessary weight on their shoulders.

How can I thank you for your sacrifice? How can I express my gratitude for my freedom? My words don't seem enough, but I thank you that you've healed and rescued me.

It's in Jesus' name I pray, amen.

*"Hear, O LORD, and have mercy on me;*
*LORD, be my helper!" You have turned for me*
*my mourning into dancing; You have put off*
*my sackcloth and clothed me with gladness.*

**PSALM 30:10–11**

F ather, you're a God of reconciliation and redemption. You are capable of more than I could ever ask or imagine.

Would you be my helper today? Turn my sadness into joy. It's so easy to stay in the depths of sadness and self-pity, but draw me out of the darkness.

Please protect my family and comfort their hearts. Show them what joy is.

Thank you that you want only the very best for us and won't leave us alone in our misery.

In Christ's name, amen.

*Hear my cry, O God; attend to my prayer.*
*From the end of the earth I will cry to*
*You, when my heart is overwhelmed; lead*
*me to the rock that is higher than I.*

PSALM 61:1–2

Father in heaven, you are the God of King David and my God too. You reign forever and over everything.

Bring me peace when I am overwhelmed. I don't know how I can accomplish all of the things I need to get done. Light my path and show me the activities and obligations I can say no to. Help me release the burdens that preoccupy my mind and keep you at bay. Come near.

God, please hear the cries of those who feel overwhelmed as they serve you. Many of them don't feel your presence right now in their lives. Remind them of your faithfulness.

Thank you for your nearness and consistency. Thank you for hearing my cries no matter where I am.

In Jesus' name, amen.

*Your sun shall no longer go down, nor shall your moon withdraw itself; for the LORD will be your everlasting light, and the days of your mourning shall be ended.*

ISAIAH 60:20

Father, you have the power to control the sun and the moon. You are the everlasting light.

Help me to see a light at the end of my tunnel. Sometimes I can barely remember what light looks like or what it feels like to have simple joy. Help me to focus on you even in the darkness.

Support my friends as they suffer losses like miscarriages, death, and illness. When these trials plague those I love, I feel so helpless. Would you show off your light in their lives?

Thank you, God, that you are our rock and healer and that you will bring our mourning to an end.

In the name of the everlasting Light, amen.

*"So I say to you, ask, and it will be given to you; seek, and you will find; knock, and it will be opened to you. For everyone who asks receives, and he who seeks finds, and to him who knocks it will be opened."*

LUKE 11:9–10

D ear God, you are ever-faithful and true to your promises. You know what we will ask before we ask it, yet you listen to your children.

I ask this day that you would open my eyes to those who are in need around me. So often I'm blind to the struggles of my friends and family, but I don't want to stay that way.

I pray for my family who needs you. Help them to ask and seek and knock, as you've promised to respond to their cries, Lord.

Thank you for answering our prayers, even when the answer is not easy to hear.

In your precious name, amen.

*Then great multitudes came to Him, having
with them the lame, blind, mute, maimed,
and many others; and they laid them down
at Jesus' feet, and He healed them.*

MATTHEW 15:30

God almighty, you are capable of healing all diseases, parting the seas, and raising the dead to life. I worship you and praise you.

Father, heal my sickness. My body aches, and my heart and my soul ache, too. Bring me relief and help me not to focus just on my own needs.

Give strength to my friends who are sick and in pain. Cradle them now and heal them.

Thank you that you hear us. Thank you that Jesus healed those who were laid before him and that you still bring healing today.

In the name of the almighty God, amen.

*Give us help from trouble, for the help of man is useless. Through God we will do valiantly, for it is He who shall tread down our enemies.*

PSALM 60:11–12

Father, you can wipe out the strongest army, move mountains, and create the earth out of nothing. Your strength and loving-kindness know no end.

Remind me of your power now. I am so quick to run to a friend for help and then feel let down. Be my strength in all situations.

My friends come to me for help sometimes, but you alone are the answer to their troubles. Help them to look to you first and always.

Thank you for being on our side and fighting for us.

In Christ's name, amen.

*And my God shall supply all
your need according to His riches
in glory by Christ Jesus.*

PHILIPPIANS 4:19

D ear Father, you meet all of our needs. You are perfect love, perfect joy, and perfect peace.

When I look to fill my needs outside of you, draw me back to you. Remind me that you are all I need. Keep me from turning to old habits and destructive patterns.

Do the same for those who are struggling with addiction. I am so afraid for them and where their lives are headed. Bring them to their knees so that they may see and know you.

Thank you that you are the God of second, third, and 100th chances. You don't give up on us.

In your name I pray this, amen.

*But I say to you, love your enemies, bless those who curse you, do good to those who hate you, and pray for those who spitefully use you and persecute you, that you may be sons of your Father in heaven.*

MATTHEW 5:44–45

Heavenly Father, your love and acceptance don't stop. You are the well of grace and love that I must draw from daily.

Help me today to love those who are hard for me to love. Humble me in their presence and show me a side of them I've been too prideful to see.

Be with those people and protect them. Whatever past pain or hurt is causing them to lash out, bring it to the surface and heal them.

Thank you for your redemptive nature and your ability to break down walls among your children.

Through Christ I pray, amen.

*You, O LORD, are a shield for me, my
glory and the One who lifts up my head.
I cried to the LORD with my voice, and
He heard me from His holy hill.*

PSALM 3:3–4

Dear God, holy and mighty one. You are
worthy of all praise, all honor. Your stead-
fast love amazes me each morning.

When I hear voices around me saying I am
not good enough, help me hear your truth in
my heart and give me strength.

Be with those who feel inadequate and doubt
if anyone cares about them. When they question
their value, give them a deeper sense of worth in
Christ, and Christ alone.

Thank you that we don't have to fight for our
worth because you have already called us your
children.

In Jesus' name, amen.

*Now then, we are ambassadors for Christ, as though God were pleading through us: we implore you on Christ's behalf, be reconciled to God. For He made Him who knew no sin to be sin for us, that we might become the righteousness of God in Him.*

2 CORINTHIANS 5:20–21

God above, you have torn the veil. You have conquered death and made a way for me to have a relationship with you.

I forget so quickly that I can talk to you anytime. Allow me to turn to you today with each step, question, and difficulty.

Surround my friends and family with your forgiveness today. Remind them that you are eager to forgive them. Help them let go of any guilt they cling to.

Thank you for making us your ambassadors on this earth.

In the name of Jesus, the One who knew no sin, amen.

*Pray without ceasing, in everything give
thanks; for this is the will of God in Christ
Jesus for you. Do not quench the Spirit.*

1 THESSALONIANS 5:17–19

Heavenly Father, I sit here in awe of all that
I should thank you for. You are so much
bigger and greater than I could ever understand.

Give me reminders to be grateful today.
Don't allow me to miss the small—or big—
blessings around me. Fill my heart with gratitude.

For my friends who struggle to pray, would
you give them a desire to know you more. Teach
them to pray, as you're teaching me to.

Thank you for Jesus. Thank you for loving
us. Thank you for the gift of grace.

In Christ's name, amen.

# 30

*And Jesus took the loaves, and when He had given thanks He distributed them to the disciples, and the disciples to those sitting down; and likewise of the fish, as much as they wanted.*

JOHN 6:11

Oh, Father, you multiply the loaves and fishes. You perform miracles that you alone are capable of. You speak all there is into being.

Help me experience your mighty power today. Show me that you are capable of more than I could ever ask or imagine. And when I see your power at work, help me be grateful for it.

I pray for everyone who feels there is not much to give thanks for right now. They have lost a child. They are sick. They have lost jobs. Fill their hearts with inexplicable gratitude, for you are still good.

I give you thanks for your almighty power and kindness. You didn't have to feed five thousand men on that hill two thousand years ago, but thank you for showing your love even through lunch.

In Jesus' name I pray, amen.

*Oh, give thanks to the LORD! Call upon
His name; make known His deeds among
the peoples! Sing to Him, sing psalms to
Him; talk of all His wondrous works!*

1 CHRONICLES 16:8–9

Father, you are so worthy of it all—my attention, praise, worship, and love. Your works are amazing, beyond anything I can even express.

Help me be a light that shines toward you today. It is often hard for me to stand out from the world and be different. Give me the courage to make your goodness known and to never be ashamed.

Please give peace to my friends who are standing up for you and as a result have found themselves friendless or with few who understand them.

I thank you for your wonderful works and all that you have done and will do.

In the glorious name of Jesus Christ, amen.

# 32

*I know that the Lord will maintain the cause of the afflicted, and justice for the poor. Surely the righteous shall give thanks to Your name; the upright shall dwell in Your presence.*

PSALM 140:12–13

Dear God, you are the true judge and the true righteous one. You are known throughout the earth.

Help me to recognize the injustice around me that I'm blind to. Help me to see my blind spots. Show me how I can help where I'm needed most.

Be with those around the world who are suffering and being taken advantage of. Raise up someone to speak on their behalf.

Thank you for being my advocate and allowing me to dwell in your presence.

In the just and righteous name of Christ, I pray this, amen.

*Then He took the cup, and when He*
*had given thanks He gave it to them,*
*and they all drank from it. And He said*
*to them, "This is My blood of the new*
*covenant, which is shed for many."*

Father, you are good. You sent your Son for us and you are merciful to us daily, moment by moment, even to the final cost.

Remind me today of your sacrifice, keep it close to my heart. Make me not only thankful for but a vessel of your grace. Don't let your grace stop with me, but show it to others through me.

Be with my friends and family who do not believe in you and have hard hearts. Let them know the promise of your good news.

Thank you for the depth of your love. You sent your Son to die a sinner's death so that I could be redeemed. Thank you that you want to have a relationship with me through Jesus Christ.

In his precious name, amen.

*Therefore I also, after I heard of your faith
in the Lord Jesus and your love for all the
saints, do not cease to give thanks for you,
making mention of you in my prayers.*

EPHESIANS 1:15–16

God, the beauty of this earth reminds me
of you. The sea, forest, and mountains
are your creation, a reflection of your power
and goodness.

I pray that you would put godly counsel in
my path. Give me the courage to seek mentor-
ship and discipleship. Don't let me depend on my
own wisdom but on yours and those wiser than I.

Be with those who have absent family members and feel abandoned. Show them that you are
their great Father who is able to fill that lonely
place.

Thank you for your faithfulness and the gift
of friendship. Thank you for bringing people
into my life to encourage me to draw near to you.

In Jesus' name, amen.

*The centurion answered and said, "Lord, I am not worthy that You should come under my roof. But only speak a word, and my servant will be healed." . . . Then Jesus said to the centurion, "Go your way; and as you have believed, so let it be done for you." And his servant was healed that same hour.*

MATTHEW 8:8,13

Good father, death is no match for you, nor sickness, nor pain. You are mightier than it all, able to abolish all suffering.

Remind me of your promises today. May I walk in them and not the promises of man. When others let me down, allow me to see your face and be comforted.

For my family, I pray you would bless them today, more than they can even ask for themselves. Surprise them at every corner and build up their faith.

Thank you that you gave us Jesus through whom all power is given. Thank you that when we ask, you hear our cries.

It's in his name that I always pray, amen.

*God, who at various times and in various*
*ways spoke in time past to the fathers*
*by the prophets, has in these last days*
*spoken to us by His Son, whom He has*
*appointed heir of all things, through*
*whom also He made the worlds.*

HEBREWS 1:1–2

My God, you are the one who spoke and still speaks. You are the one who came and still comes.

Give me a discerning heart toward the Holy Spirit. Teach me to hear. Teach me to be still and silent to know when you are talking. Give me silence today.

Point my friends and family in the direction of your truth. As they are trying to decide which way to go, give them the strength to choose your way above their own.

Thank you for the hope we have in you and that we have eternity to look forward to.

In the name of the Son, who is heir to all things, amen.

*Therefore God also has highly exalted Him
and given Him the name which is above
every name, that at the name of Jesus every
knee should bow, of those in heaven, and of
those on earth, and of those under the earth.*

**PHILIPPIANS 2:9–10**

F ather, your name is above all other names.
You deserve my worship and my praise.

Help me to remember that the same power
that conquered the grave also lives in me. So
often I take for granted what Christ did for me.
Teach me the truths of Jesus as if I am hearing
them for the first time.

Please help my friends and family to see that
your way is righteous and true.

Thank you, God, that you give us what we
need when we need it.

In Christ's name, amen.

*They shall neither hunger anymore nor thirst anymore; the sun shall not strike them, nor any heat; for the Lamb who is in the midst of the throne will shepherd them and lead them to living fountains of waters. And God will wipe away every tear from their eyes.*

REVELATION 7:16–17

Dear God, only you take away pain and suffering. You lift our burdens and bring comfort in your perfect timing.

Keep my eyes heavenward. When my thoughts stray to worry about the future or regret the past, lift my eyes up so that I will focus on the ultimate goal.

Bring freedom to my friends, who are living in and regretting their pasts. Give them the strength to let go and remind them that you will wipe every tear from their eyes.

Thank you for sending your Son to us and quenching all of our thirsts. And thank you for fulfilling all of your promises.

In the name of the Living Water, amen.

*Then Peter said, "Silver and gold
I do not have, but what I do have I
give you: In the name of Jesus Christ
of Nazareth, rise up and walk."*

A<small>CTS</small> 3:6

Heavenly Father, your kindness has no limits and your mercy is abundant, over-flowing in my life. You are not stingy with your grace and sympathy.

Some days I feel like I don't even have the strength to stand. Would you pick me up and give me the power to make it through those times?

Please help my friends, who are also struggling. When their hearts are heavy and their hands are weary, lift them up through your good name.

Thank you that the name of Jesus has the power to make the lame walk and to give sight to the blind. And it has the power to help me through every trial I face.

In the name of Jesus, all powerful and all compassionate, amen.

*And Jesus came and spoke to them,
saying, "All authority has been given to
Me in heaven and on earth. Go therefore
and make disciples of all the nations,
baptizing them in the name of the Father
and of the Son and of the Holy Spirit."*

MATTHEW 28:18–19

Father, you are good. You love all of your people with a love I'll never fully understand. You care for each child in each nation and know every heart.

Give me the desire to spread your word. I so often keep it quiet. Let it begin to burn in me in a way that I can do nothing but tell others of your love and glory.

Be with my friends who are missionaries and working in other countries to share the good news of the gospel. Let them be encouraged and built up today.

Thank you for your love and for calling me to be a part of sharing it with the world.

In Jesus' name, amen.

# Discover Even More Power in a Simple Prayer

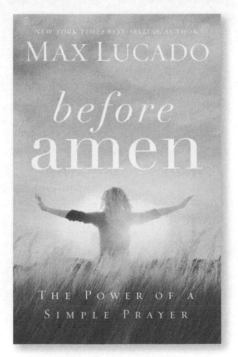

ISBN 978-0-8499-4848-0
$19.99

Join Max Lucado on a journey to the very heart of biblical prayer and discover rest in the midst of chaos and confidence even for prayer wimps.

*Available wherever books are sold.*

BeforeAmen.com

# Make Your Prayers Personal

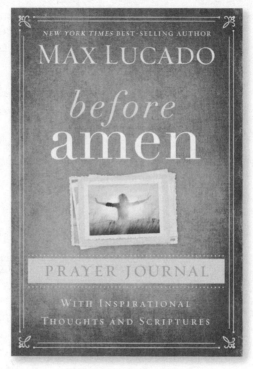

ISBN 978-0-7180-1406-3

$13.99

This beautiful companion journal to *Before Amen* helps readers stoke their prayer life. It features quotes and scriptures to inspire both prayer warriors and those who struggle to pray.

# Tools for Your Church and Small Group

## Before Amen: A DVD Study

ISBN 978-0-529-12342-8

$21.99

Max Lucado leads this four-session study through his discovery of a simple tool for connecting with God each day. This study will help small group participants build their prayer life, calm the chaos of their world, and grow in Christ.

## Before Amen Study Guide

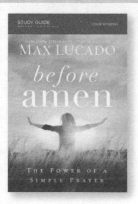

ISBN 978-0-529-12334-3

$9.99

This guide is filled with Scripture study, discussion questions, and practical ideas designed to help small-group members understand Jesus' teaching on prayer. An integral part of the *Before Amen* small-group study, it will help group members build prayer into their everyday lives.

# *Before Amen*
# Church Campaign Kit

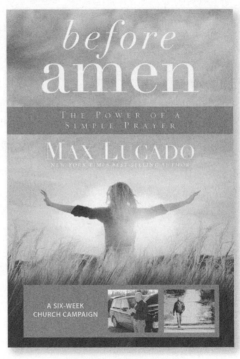

ISBN 978-0-529-12369-5

$49.99

The church campaign kit includes a four-session DVD study by Max Lucado; a study guide with discussion questions and video notes; the *Before Amen* trade book; a getting started guide; and access to a website with all the sermon resources churches need to launch and sustain a four-week *Before Amen* campaign.

# Before Amen for Everyone

## Before Amen Audiobook

ISBN 978-1-4915-4662-8

$19.99

Enjoy the unabridged audio CD of *Before Amen*.

## Before Amen eBook

ISBN 978-0-529-12390-9

$19.99

Read *Before Amen* anywhere on your favorite tablet or electronic device.

## Antes del amén Spanish Edition

ISBN 978-0-7180-0157-5

$13.99

The hope of *Before Amen* is also available for Spanish-language readers.

# before amen

## a worship collection

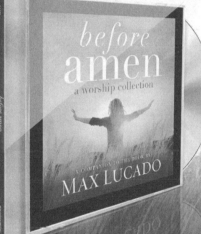

**BEFORE AMEN: A WORSHIP COLLECTION** is a perfect worship and prayer companion to the book *Before Amen*. Touching on each chapter within the book, these songs further enhance your prayer and devotional times, while helping you memorize and internalize each of the book's themes. The artists featured on this album represent some of the top names in Christian music.

**CD: $13.99**  UPC: 000768629628
**DIGITAL: $9.99**  UPC: 000768629659

INTEGRITY MUSIC
THE SOUND OF WORSHIP

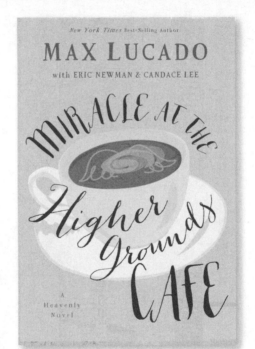

# Make Prayer a Daily Part of Your Child's Life

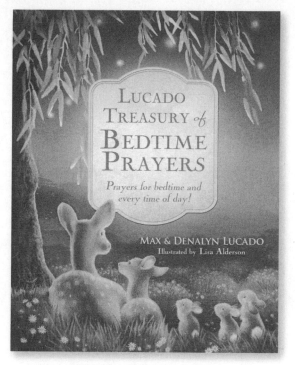

*Coming January 2015*

ISBN 978-0-7180-1631-9
$19.99

Featuring brand new prayers from Max and Denalyn Lucado alongside classics adapted especially for young readers, the *Lucado Treasury of Bedtime Prayers* will help children begin a lifelong conversation with God.

# GOD REDEEMED THE STORY OF JOSEPH.
# CAN'T HE REDEEM YOUR STORY AS WELL?

you'll
get
through
this

HOPE AND HELP FOR YOUR TURBULENT TIMES

# MAX LUCADO
New York Times Best-Selling Author

God is in the business of redeeming the broken. He was for Joseph.
He is still. Do you crave some hope for these tough times?
Then this is the message you need.

MaxLucado.com

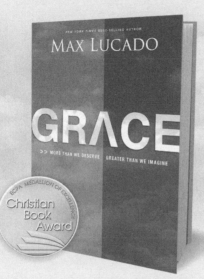